1,000 Roads to Discovery

Kia Amy Woods

Copyright © 2017 Kia Amy Woods

Edited by Jennifer Niter
Cover by Barbara Broadnax & Katelyn Nettles

All rights reserved.

ISBN: 0996670319

ISBN-13: 978-0996670319

Dedication

Anyone who has chosen art as a form of release as opposed to malice. To anyone who has chosen love as opposed to hatred.

To anyone who has chosen growth and resilience as opposed to playing the victim. To anyone who has worked to break the cycle, this one is for you.

Contents

	Acknowledgments	vii
	Note to the Reader	ix
1	Communication	3
2	Discrimination	9
3	Love, Heartbreak & Healing	19
4	Insecurities & Self-doubt	37
5	Self-worth	47
6	Forgiveness, Friendships & Family	55
7	Self-care	63
8	Strength & Resilience	75
9	Growth & Wisdom	81
10	Discovery	87
	About the Author	97

Preview:
Positive Reinforcement: Daily Declarations
by Kia Amy Woods

Acknowledgements

Thank you to all of the readers and supporters of my first book **Positive Reinforcement: Daily Declarations**. Thank you for allowing me the opportunity to inspire you and others. Thank you for giving the gift of positivity to those that purchased it for others or passed it on. I am pleased that you have returned for a second dose of creativity.

For those that asked about and anticipated the second book, I am humbled by you. I appreciate you tremendously, and I hope I live up to your expectation.

To each and every member of my support system, I thank you.

Carysma Smith & Felicia Bray, I am eternally grateful that I had you in my life as a teenager. You were role models and now are my sisters!

Tas and Ashley, there is nothing I wouldn't do for you. Your lives have truly made mine worth living, even during my darkest hour.
My heart beats for you.

Parents, my goal is to make you proud.

Note to the Reader

There are reoccurring themes and lessons I have experienced in my short lifetime. Throughout childhood, adolescence and adulthood, I have lived days that make up the content of this body of work. I once read that a lesson will repeat itself until it is learned. That repetition was crucial to survival, healing, self-care, and expression. While these are my thoughts, experiences and the way I choose to express myself, I am confident that I do not stand alone in anything you will read. There are some things that put me on edge when while writing. There may be some content that will put you on edge. I recommend you review and censor before sharing with children.

While many things are written to women or from a woman's perspective, I have intersectional intentions. I begin with some of the more difficult and controversial topics and move into what I have done to cope and to grow from all that I have encountered. This book was written over the course of 13 years, so you may notice a change in perspective and spirituality. My path has changed many times. Along the way, I learned that discovery is not a destination or a religion, but the journey itself. Here are my 1,000 roads discovery, I invite you to join me in my travels. Some of the poetry in this book can be found on *Soundcloud.com/Kia-Woods*

1
Communication

2016

Think of the person that you find easiest to talk to. Think of who you can confide in whether you have made a mistake, are being irrational or have improvements to make. Think of how they speak to you. Your inner voice should mirror theirs. Be gentle with yourself. Love yourself despite your flaws. Aspire to begin again with newly acquired wisdom. Be your own best friend.

2015

You are responsible for the energy you put into the universe.

2017

Effective communication can make a difference between a continuation and a finale.

2016

Emotional intelligence is something we should all aspire to. The same way knowledge proves to be useful in many situations, knowing how and when to respond to things can greatly influence a positive outcome. We often act out of emotion, leaving logic out of the equation. Those actions in turn may cause emotional reactions from others. What a different place the world would be if we didn't allow our emotions to rule us. As you continue to face challenges, allow the wisdom from the past to lead the way.

2015

The most difficult things to say are usually the things that need to be said the most. Seek courage and move forward in honesty.

2016

Make sure you aren't just hearing them, but truly listening.

2015

If you ask the universe for a sign, be prepared that it may not be what you were hoping for. Be cognizant of ignoring red flags sent your way simply because they aren't what you anticipated.

2014

There is a voice inside of you that cautions you. Listen intently to that voice. It is your intuition. It is there to protect you.

■ ■ ■ ■ ■

2015

Wellness is being aligned mind, body and spirit. With knowledge that the preservation of our total being is necessary for healthy existence, it becomes our duty to take a holistic approach in our self-care routines. We must listen to each part of ourselves with a level of understanding that can only come from mastering this alignment.

■ ■ ■ ■ ■

2015

We don't have a choice in who our soul connects with. It is a predetermined arrangement made before the start of this lifetime. Whether we acknowledge or ignore our soul mates, we will undoubtedly be drawn to them. We should make the most of these encounters. Identifying members of our soul family is the way we find bright spots in our darkest hours.

Communication Mantra

Energy flows to and from me freely.

I am open and in alignment.

2
Discrimination

2015

I look forward to a day where it's not necessary to remind the world "Black lives matter" because the life of every human being will be seen as what it is first and foremost, a human life.
I wait for a day that people do not feel upset, threatened or intimidated by our pride because loving ourselves doesn't mean we hate others.
A day where openly expressing favor toward our culture and traditions will be seen only as an acknowledgement that we too, are deserving of favor. The day there is no need to highlight black history exclusively, as it will be celebrated and included in our world history lessons.

Yes, I look forward to this day I am not sure I will see in my lifetime. While I wait, I will remain hopeful, head held high and exuding my pride. I'll create, lead, shine, love, educate, promote peace, forgive, and live my Black history.

■ ■ ■ ■ ■

2017

We blame ourselves for the things we are unable to control. We find ourselves robbed of our truths because we are trying to placate others. It somehow has become the job of the victim to comfort those who find discomfort in the pain they have caused us.
We apologize repeatedly for our valid feelings.
We are told that we must forgive.
We are told that we must heal.
It is rare that we are given the room to be angry. To be unapologetically frustrated about the unfortunate circumstances we face.
Suggestions that we get over it, stop whining and move on are insulting, yet we are so used to it, we have found ways to tolerate and be civil.
Our reflections aren't convenient.
Our opinions are too strong. With our rage stifled our oppression is never ending.

■ ■ ■ ■ ■

2017

The biggest threat to white privilege is Black power.

2003

I Am
(Written at age 16)

I am 16 years of unspoken words.
A victim of this cruel world with a voice unheard.
I am too young to be wise. An example of a teenager that has never been taught better.
That's what I am in your eyes.
The truth is I am full of hostility trying my best to be civil.
I am my brothers and sisters that don't say a word as old ladies pull their purses closer as we get on the train.
I am the pain felt by many caused by a racial slur or the hatred directed toward us because of the color of our skin.
I am an outcast trying to fit in.
And I am whatever you DON'T say I am because you will never speak the truth about me and will never see me as anything more than a black girl from the hood with farfetched dreams.
I am judged and labeled by a stereotype instead of by my undeniable intelligence and my willingness to learn.
I am the perfect example of a girl that doesn't need the aid of hair weave and press on nails to feel beautiful.
I am the tears of every mother that has outlived a child who chose the streets as a way of life.
I am the hatred and fear of every young girl that has had her innocence taken away by some

pervert who is the reason why she'll never trust a man again.
I am every ounce of pain felt by my brothers when the bullets pierce their skin.
Bullets shot by a white cop that never went to trial.
Murder labeled an accident.
I am the heart of every young lady that doesn't seem to understand that if she needs to degrade herself to be popular, she should be keeping different company.
I am the envy of the brown skin second graders that look at their fairer skin peers and feel jealous because society has forgotten to teach them that black is beautiful, even if the month has more than 28 days.
I am the heartache of every child that has seen their fathers walk out of the door and out of their lives.
I am the confused feelings of the innocent children that are going to grow up in this crazy world unsure of who they are and who they want to become.
I am every suicide attempt made by young people that no longer appreciate the precious gift of life and has chosen the cowardly out.
I am a volcano full of emotions ready to erupt at any given time without a single warning.
Sick and tired of trying to make people understand my heart, my soul and everything that I am!

2017

For anyone that has grown tired of hearing about social injustices and racial tension, imagine how it would feel if for over 400 years, you and your people had to live it. What appears to be bitterness is sometimes caution. Don't allow denial and naivety to cause you to behave in a way that will be received as insensitivity by those affected the most.

2017

The division among the oppressed is how the oppressors stay in power. If you have been a victim of racism, sexism, classism, ableism, homophobia, transphobia, xenophobia and belief-based bigotry, it is important that you understand that we are all on the same team.

2017

When intersectionality becomes our reality we will not only survive, but we will thrive.

2016

Suffering is so familiar to many of us that we become desensitized to it. We are often exposed to toxicity at an early age. We begin to expect it and believe it is normal. Walking through fire is something we become comfortable with.
No one has ever taught us that we do not have to accept abuse. We are not taught that we are allowed to be healthy. We are not encouraged to break the cycle.

2006

What happened to the girl worth fighting for?
She wants to see the day her efforts are accepted with the promise of reciprocity.
She wants to believe her heart is not too big, nor eyes too blind to accept what appears to be her reality.
What happened to the girl worth fighting for?
Has she been smothered by a dream? Buried in the darkness or burned by the sun?
Have the multiple attempts at discovering who she really is caused her to hide even further by sinking into her shell?
She's gravely misjudged, underestimated and misunderstood. She's also by definition, imperfect and frequently misunderstands. She reinvents herself in order to gain continued self-acceptance.
Once in a while she finds herself exposed, only to eventually be given a reason to once again retreat.
What happened to the girl worth fighting for?

She has gotten lost in a dark hole somewhere deep inside of me.

■ ■ ■ ■ ■

2017

We are strength like it has never been defined.
A union that has yet to be identified.
We are the marginalized. We are the forgotten souls. Our names will be embedded in history long after social media introduces a new hashtag. Our blood stains the streets. The pain doesn't dissipate. We wait for a new headline and wonder how many names don't make the news. We hope, we fight, we march and we boycott for the right to simply live.
Remember our names. Hear our voices. We will not be silenced. We will not be erased!

■ ■ ■ ■ ■

2017

Hatred isn't innate. It is learned behavior meant to oppose love, unity and everything that is pure.

Discrimination Mantra

We will not be silenced. We will not be erased.

3
Love, Heartbreak & Healing

2016

Touched
(Audio on soundcloud.com/Kia-Woods)

You said hello to my heart before you ever spoke a word. Wrapped up in your existence prior to fully being exposed, I'm here.
Magic, power, kismet...it's one thing, it's something. It's all of the above.
I do not know what I cannot process.
I download your face in my mind and my heart smiles for a little while and then needs a refresher. Your words save the day, making up for each moment I've lacked in my entire life.

They are spoken as if they are delivered to and for me.
Dissect, research, process and repeat.
I've had a lifetime of homework and you are my favorite assignment.
Lifted off of the ground and submerged simultaneously, I can't make sense of it. Nothing is what it used to be.
I'm supposed to be; growing, learning; loving, prepared for a moment I never really thought would come.
Companionship served as a pacifier and temporarily eased my mind.
My soul unfulfilled and restless as it awaited a special union.
Serial lover I've found in you and want to know how I am different.
What sets me apart inside of that open heart you so freely give and give and give again.
My soul made a promise to yours once or maybe it was the other way around. Not sure when and where, but I have this now.
Who I used to be pleases me, but I know I am forever changed.
Energies exchanged, you tell me I'm yours. Ready or not, I don't have to agree but can't deny chemistry and what's supposed to be, inevitably, incredibly. I am lost.
I have searched my world for translation. I haven't spoken a word of a language that's familiar to me.
My favorite mystery, I'm challenged.
Guarded, hard and scarred, I am done healing.

I am NOT done healing.
And it doesn't seem to matter.
You've arrived like a new day. An appointment previously made.
Another life, I was your wife, and this is the sequel.
I have yet to touch you and yet I feel you. I've heard you but I've not received.
I am filled with fear of what could go so right.
I am curious, I am open, I am not in control.
It was you. It is you...it's always been you…
Said hello to my heart before ever speaking a word.

Eternity
(Audio on soundcloud.com/Kia-Woods)

Where have you been? With every fiber of my being, I breathe you.
With every sense I receive you.
Fear has been evicted and left no return address.
I am open.
I have not, will not, nor do I expect to suddenly possess the ability to express myself.
I am speechless.
Each breath I take you in. I hold my breath so I can hold you in.
Love my life even more so that I can love you in.
An angel sitting on my shoulder tells me to let you in.
To receive a gift from above. To cherish true love and I cannot disappoint her.
So again I ask where have you been?
Your references to divine timing allow my brain and heart to momentarily synchronize and I sit still for a while and just breathe.
My gift from God I shall not take for granted. I will not walk away.
This world will see a woman gone mad and I will properly, gladly and openly introduce myself.
I'll lovingly be whomever they want me to be as long as I can be.....with you.
Time lapses and eternity now has meaning as I look into your eyes.

You switched gears and my former direction now becomes unclear, you've just become the conductor of my fantasy ride.
No need for a safe belt. I'm headed to where I'm headed and I'll arrive in the state I was meant to.
Divine intervention has now been explained when I realize that previous plans are null and void.
No heartbreak even matters and I thank them for releasing you.
For growing you, building you and preparing you.
It's time for me to take over but not before I thank them for hurting me.
For leaving me and for deceiving me.
Had it not been for the pain I've suffered I may not have known,
I WOULD not have known that my life could change every day in every way.
Too big for this world, I want to love you in outer space.
My love, you are worth every one of my years and every one of my tears, I promise you.
What they failed to deliver is irrelevant, because as place warmers they were never meant to succeed.
Taking my rightful place on the throne beside you, I'm ready.
Release, forgive, and wish well. No bitterness. I am thankful.
Every former lover has given us a gift.
They have made room in our lives for this moment. I've been waiting.

Where have you been? I've been anxious.
Started to believe you didn't exist, but remained patient.
My body shivers right in this moment as I feel you in my spirit.
It's involuntary; I want to love you ON PURPOSE.
Share your world, close my eyes, be free and feel.
Give birth to your child, live here for a while and then begin again next lifetime.
Hear me now, universe I thank you.
Explosive collision meant for the history books. I am honored.
One half of this plan, I am equipped.
Every hardship, every success, every exchange of energy has prepared me for you.
Moving forward to reach you they will have to go through me, only because I am apart of you.
Another heart has been introduced and we are beating together as one.
Where have you been? The answer is now clear you were here.
Present when I looked in the mirror, as you are my reflection.
Present when I felt empty yet kept going, as you are my strength.
Present when I was yearning and deprived, as you are my nourishment.
Present when I've been burned and forgiven, as you are my love.
Present when I've not believed but still achieved, as you are my motivation.

You've been with me my entire life as I carried you in my spirit until the day I would meet your physical form.
What a pleasure it has been and if you do not mind, I would like to continue with you by my side.
Would you consider moving with me into eternity?

Exposed
(Audio on soundcloud.com/Kia-Woods)

One day I woke up to find I wasn't wearing any clothing.
I'd been shed of my armor, my sword and shield lay on the ground.
Caught up in the moment like one of those fairytales.
I went to bed and forgot to use protection.
This senseless decision left me in an unfavorable position.
I forgot to be vigilant. I lost myself in the thought of love.
Mutual, consensual, earth shattering love.
Something I would do on purpose and with pleasure.
Started day dreaming of what could and would be.
My duties as one half of a new union only excited me.
My reality, though frightening, left a sweet after taste behind.
Still, I wanted to take my time, pull the covers up and hide because no one likes being exposed.
Searching for some relief as day turned into night.
Began to feel cheated, violated and insecure.
Instead of shelter, darkness only produced additional fear.
Confirmation that there are consequences to getting carried away.

I used to believe that I'd rather lose anything else than to lose what guarded me.
What I used to believe doesn't help at all right now.
Memories serve as soft internal whispers reminding me why there is always a need to pack extra just in case.
This way, you never find yourself empty and alone.
Decisions are not exactly mine, as I am simply a passenger on this ride, a victim of time.
Nonsensical are the thoughts that are too invasive. I do not recognize this person that looks all too familiar. She takes a back seat to the woman in me that has taken charge again and is determined to find her clothing. Searching diligently for her body armor. Knows she placed a shield somewhere.
Determined to no longer be vulnerable.
Somewhere out there lives happily ever after stories.
Ones that have two people in love together more often that they are apart.
Somewhere out there a woman trusts a true love with her heart.
That somewhere out there is not in here.
All that continues to dwell is constant fear.
One day I woke up to find I wasn't wearing any clothing.
I'd been stripped of my armor, my sword and shield lay on the ground.
Though I've tried to adjust, I'm uncomfortable.

I'm not in control. I am scared. I am tired of fearing and waiting for the unknown.
I want my strength. I crave my power.
Searching for the clothing and armor that once protected me has been exhausting. Though I've retrieved bits and pieces, the uniform doesn't fit the same.
I'll continue this internal battle because my restless mind will never allow it to end.
It has taken some time but I think I finally understand.
All I have to offer now is everything I am.

2013

I Choose Me

Someone had to take the pain away so I chose you. Actually it was you who chose me. I sat around unknowingly, an unsuspecting soul. A heart with no room left for anything but additional confusion. It was simply unavailable, but still it chose you.
Somehow I had to make sense of this and someone had to have the answers, so I chose you. If there were ever a time I would allow myself to be called a victim, it would be times when I was all in. All in with my heart out and eyes closed. All in.....alone.
Somewhere lays the secret of how to erase you from my mind. How to allow my heart to grasp the fact that more days has passed since you left my life than the sum of the days you were in it. That time frame should ease the pain. Blurred memories should not lead to emotion so vivid. So crisp, so true. Someone has to provide an escape and I chose you.
Someday I have to learn that each of my choices is what led me here in the first place. I have to find the strength to do what I'm not used to doing, what I have neglected to. I have to choose me. I have to find courage deep within. Resilience left over from pass tribulation, and forgiveness I offer to everyone except myself. I need to forgive myself for still craving what has proven to be

anything but mine. For not having my all to give anyone else.
I need someone to love, to cherish, to make me whole. I need someone to stop choosing you.
Today I choose...me.

2017

Irony has been defined when the person that is praying for you is the same person that has caused irreparable disruption to your peace in the first place.
Don't take advantage of her kindness and generosity, play on her vulnerability and borrow from her strength while allowing your mediocrity to be a sinking weight to her and then pray for her healing.
Instead, recognize upfront when you have nothing to add to her magic, keep your distance and wish her well as she continues to rise in power like the Queen she is.
Then and only then will you have done her a favor.
Then and only then will you have truly shown her love.

2015

So many things in life are mediocre. Love shouldn't be one of them.

Rebirth

2015

You fell in love with the thought of me. You were apparently captivated by the idea of who I appeared to be.
I was a quest you set out to conquer. What you failed to realize is that you were never equipped to handle the reality of all that comes with a multi-dimensional being.
I played the game and I continued to fool myself. I forgot that my life and happiness was my responsibility. The pleasure my presence brought you was conditional. My personality was too strong, my voice too loud, my black too proud.
So I hid.
Hid away to fall in line with the rest of suburbia. I blended in to the best of my ability.
Told myself it was time to grow up. I heard all of the voices telling me that it was time to settle down.
I could get my fuel at a rest stop along the way. Everyone can't be everything to everyone.
I knew that and so I dreamed of exciting conversations that could awake my sleeping spirit.
Something that would require me to use my voice.
I fought constantly against dimming my own light and still I did it anyway.
I didn't realize that this internal battle was indication enough that I wasn't where I needed to be.

Slowly I felt the inner me dying...crying as she suffocated.
In time, I was reborn. Vowed to never again allow the best parts of me to be murdered by what another person wants me to be.

■ ■ ■ ■ ■

2014

Love means trying to understand what is not easily understood.
Putting your feelings aside at times to ensure there is room to empathize.
It means sometimes trying your best to be perfect, knowing you are taking on an impossible task.
Love means acknowledging when you've fallen short, and never being too proud to ask forgiveness.
Love means sharing concerns.
Speaking with words unspoken and loving even when pieces have been broken. Loving me means that you will experience my failed attempts at perfection.
It means you'll witness me fall short.
To love one another means to proceed knowing that actions are not always a reflection of intent. To have confidence that our love is strong enough to withstand any misunderstanding and so powerful it can be renewed on command.

■ ■ ■ ■ ■

2015

How many of us have been in relationships or situations we knew were not meant for us just because we were scared to be alone? We don't want to start over or we are afraid of being lonely.

We cling tightly to toxicity because in our minds, that's better than the unknown.

If you're in love with who you are, being alone doesn't automatically equate to loneliness.

Have the courage to get to know who you truly are. If for some reason you're unable to love something about your character, it's your responsibility to work full time to change it.

I would rather be a woman who spends her entire life, in search of passion, depth, and excellence to match what I offer, than to live a life where I have accepted the idea of being unfulfilled.

One of the most beautiful things is life is to love and be loved unconditionally.

As human beings it is natural to desire romance and companionship. But before any hopes of happily ever after, YOU should be the love of your life.

If you don't find true love for within, you'll always need the company of another to feel whole.

And even then you'll likely realize that you don't truly feel whole at all.

You may feel content, you may grow fond of routines and begin to rely on the company of

another person, but something will always be missing.
You may have feelings of "this will do" and mistake it for love.
You see others in love around you, and you may feel happy to have someone by your side so that you can fit in.
If anything I have said sounds familiar, now is the time to make a change.
It's time to be brave enough to be your own best friend, your own strength and your own support system. Do not sell yourself short and settle simply out of fear of being alone.

■ ■ ■ ■ ■

2015

Don't be so afraid of getting to know yourself that you find it absolutely necessary to constantly be on the hunt for happiness in the arms of another.
Do not expect someone to fulfill a piece of you that you are unable to fulfill yourself.
Seek substance within or forever remain empty.

Love, Heartbreak & Healing Mantra

All of the love I need already lives within. I have fallen in love with me.

4
Insecurities & Self-doubt

2013

Suicide - *Reflections of abused teenager*
Special Thank You to my little sister Tas, who is my hero in more ways than one.

I've had enough. I don't understand why nothing in life goes the way it was designed to. I don't understand why God's blessings seem to reject me as my parents fail to protect me.
I don't understand what he sees in me. Or he, or him either. I live this life in a tiny frame. Not a curve in sight. Provocative attire and salacious desires are foreign to me, and still I am the chosen one. Over and over I am...chosen.
When does this end? How can I make it stop? I don't want to figure out why me, as I continue to figure out what it takes to be a decent human being and a role model for my sisters. I don't

want to wonder what I am doing wrong or what I could've done differently. I don't want this responsibility, I didn't ask for this life.
Stepping into a place designed for a mother means I'm subject to behavior only intended for a woman.
I can end this myself. I can take this away. I can fade into nothingness and be at peace.
Or will I be? Will I forever be punished? Will God show me mercy knowing I simply have had more than I can possibly bear?
As I sit here, wondering, contemplating, shaking and feeling as though I'm suffocating, I feel like he has answered me.
And then suddenly, she's there, she's crying and she says no. She removes the knife from my hand. The fear in her eyes lets me know I was selfish to think of leaving her behind. The vision enters my mind and I think of how I would've surely left her traumatized. I promise her that though this has happened before, it will never happen again. I don't plan to break my promise to someone who saved my life.

2015

Be limitless in a world that wants nothing more but to cage you. Be a rebel!

2012

If you truly want something, pursue it wholeheartedly. Do not back down from anything or anyone. Not even the voice in your head that appears during moments of uncertainty. Remind yourself that self-doubt is the recipe for failure.

2016

She carries herself not like she's flawless, but like she's a Goddess, and that means even her flaws are beautiful.

2014

There was a time when I avoided mirrors. It was once a habit to point out flaws on sight. I was my toughest critic and I told myself it had to be that way. I thought that if I had an awareness of all of my unattractive features I could shield myself from others when they became aware. It wasn't until recently that I realized I was inflicting self-harm. I was the toxicity that I was trying to avoid in others.

2016

Reminder: Their approval is NOT required.

2016

Ambition activated by hard work will ultimately defeat self-doubt.

Letter To My Childhood Abusers

Time usually fades memories, allows for distance between a past reality & expectations for the present. These scars of mine are stronger than the time meant to heal them. Visibility to the average onlooker is minimal, but every night, every touch, every new relationship, every new light, means I have to again face the horror I will forever be trying to escape.

The mirror reveals a woman that is determined to be strong. As a little girl an idol by the name of Whitney made her believe "no matter what they take from me, they can't take away my dignity."

What happens when false dignity is all you have left? How does dignity pair with a pool of insecurities?

Have you taken the best part of me? Will I ever love myself honestly?

Innocence of my childhood belongs to a man, or two, can't forget about the third.

Cries for help went unheard. Certain it was me, has to be when violation occurs repeatedly.

When does it stop, when does it… STOP!

Stop your hurting, stop your tears…it's been forever don't give them anymore years. The bruises, the scars, can be covered…hidden. But a broken woman will never escape the stares…and everyone will know he has won.

Misplaced blame and anger. Disguised very well. When most people around can't even tell. When they are impressed at your strides, admire your strength, it makes you feel that you, may actually just be worthy.
Bent, broken, but not destroyed. I should find a blessing, I should seek joy. Have faith in all I am and all that aspire to be. The Godly thing to do would be to forgive you for the life you took from me, the pride you destroyed, the explanations I've since had to give and the days I didn't want to live. The person they think I am, has already forgiven, practically forgotten. Doesn't stare in their faces looking for you. I know you are out there, & this time you won't catch me off guard. Paranoia has officially set in because when I search, I find. In every face, I can see yours if I look deep enough. I can feel you if I'm touched long enough. I can hear you if I listen closely enough. So why can't I erase you if I wash long enough? Forgive you if I pray hard enough? Burn you if despite how you've weakened me, I've proven strong enough?
You dictated who I was and it's like I can never prove you wrong enough.
It's time I talk to the little girl that hides within me. I will comfort her and nurture her, tend to her wounds. Show her how to be selective, teach her to trust, but that her trust is a gift. Be her strength, her fire, protection from each blow. As for forgiveness, I'll be honest & say that something, she may never know.

2016

A quitting mentality can be a healthy one if you are abandoning the right things.

2015

How many times have you doubted yourself and yet expected others to believe in you?
If you haven't convinced yourself of your abilities it will be difficult to convince others.
Get to know who you are and what you are good at. Be the captain of your own cheerleading squad. Once you have total faith in yourself, you are unstoppable!

Insecurities & Self Doubt Mantra

Self-doubt is a recipe for failure. I believe in all that I am and what I am capable of.

5
Self-worth

2015

You will discover those that aren't equipped to handle all that you are and what you have to offer. Others will be outright intimidated by your beauty, intellect, talent and strength. Don't you dare hide your superpowers or conform to mediocrity. Accept that you may be too strong for some. View it as a compliment. If you aren't an acquired taste, you're way too common. Aim higher!

2015

Like any rare gem, a good woman cannot be afforded by just anyone. Not everyone that is interested can indulge. Some will admire from the window and pray for the means to one day get lucky. Others will apprehensively approach, hoping for a chance experience her, if only for a moment. Many will be turned away because rare gems never belong to just anyone. A select few will have the privilege of getting close but will ultimately be intimidated by that kind of exclusivity. There will be some that recognize that they must hold on to this gem and that is what they will do for a while, but may make the mistake of putting it down when they become preoccupied. Like any rare gem that's been shelved, a good woman will eventually be discovered by someone that can afford her and appreciates the privilege. The ones that once had this gem in their possession learn a harsh lesson. Don't ever place a treasure down while you continue to shop around. You will likely come back one day to see that this treasure is no longer available to you.

2015

Being a woman is one of the most amazing, powerful, exhilarating, fascinating, and beautiful gifts.

Women: We give the gift of life. We run businesses and take care of home simultaneously. We fight for the people we love, even after they have hurt us. We rally and protest for what we believe in. When we are viewed as second rate and are under paid, we still give our all because we take pride in our work. We are stronger than we give ourselves credit for.
We are role models, intellectuals, educators, creators, innovators and artists.

Note to my fellow woman: If you are living a life where you aren't cherished, please consider making different decisions. Do not allow anyone in your life that doesn't treat you like a Queen. You deserve to be fulfilled!

2015

Physical beauty isn't an accomplishment. It is merely a matter of genetics. Strive to have an attractive aura, mind, soul, and spirit to match.

2015

Value yourself enough to be intentionally progressive. Fall in love with YOU. Until you know how to truly love, invest in, trust, forgive and be good to yourself, you cannot do those things for others.

2017

You my darling, are a rose. If they cannot handle your thorns, they do not deserve access to your garden.

2017

Never hide your magic simply because it threatens others. Do not let anyone else dictate who you are supposed to be. Sometimes people decide you are "too much" because they simply aren't enough. Your self worth should not be tied to another person's insecurities.

2015

Some of the most difficult moments in life include transitioning from who you are into who were meant to be. The journey to your highest self may be a lonely one.

2014

Write your remarkable legacy with carefully selected words and actions. The encounters you have today determine the memories you leave behind tomorrow.

Self-worth Mantra

*As I have learned to love myself,
I have become aware that my self-worth
isn't dependent on the validation of others.*

6
Forgiveness, Friendships & Family

2014

Forgiveness is crucial to healing. It is something you should not only do for yourself but for others. We are granted grace daily. We should remember when we think of denying others of requested forgiveness.

Forgiveness does not mean that we must go on as if we have never been hurt.

It is not only acceptable but wise, to remain vigilant and protective of our heart and feelings. You do not have to expose yourself to the same person(s) or circumstance that lead to painful events.

In an effort to self-preserve; forgive others, forgive yourself and move on protected in newly acquired wisdom.

◾ ◾ ◾ ◾ ◾

2016

Surround yourself with people that encourage and/or cultivate your skills, talents, determination, intellect, passion, drive, depth and creativity. Keeping company that is not conducive to your personal development and the expansion of your mindset hinders and distracts you from reaching your full potential. It doesn't take long for you to settle for a new normal that will ultimately stunt your growth. Choose your team wisely. Don't waste time that could be spent building an empire on things or individuals that do not have what it takes to dwell amongst royalty. If you aren't progressing you aren't living.

◾ ◾ ◾ ◾ ◾

2016

Often times the raw truth is difficult to accept. Whether it's from the voice inside or from another person, we generally want to believe in ourselves and in those we have chosen to be around us. We want to believe we have good judgment. We believe that if we are able to form a strong bond with someone, they must be a quality person. We aren't always willing to accept the fact that we all need work. At times we have lapses in judgement and allow people to get close to us that should have remained at a distance.

2015

Wish no harm to those who have harmed you. Remember that people trying to break others are usually broken themselves. This does not mean you should subject yourself to additional pain from them. Separate yourself for the sake of protection but do not hate or be vindictive. Pray for the healing of the person instead. You will find peace you never thought possible.

2016

Let your words be a reflection of your heart and your actions a reflection of your words. If you care, tell them. If you love them, show it. Tomorrow is not promised to any of us. Cherish those you love each day and ensure they know they are valued.

2015

Gentle reminder: Learn to forgive. It is how you sleep peacefully at night and wake up without hatred in your heart.

2017

Note to parents:
When you are done raising your children the rest of the world still has to deal with them. Even after they have moved out and on with their lives, they will be friends, partners, neighbors, students, teachers, mentors, coaches, businessmen/women, etc. Keep that in mind while planting the seeds that will flourish into their skill set, behavior and attitude. Be diligent, intentional, and thorough. Handle with care and teach them well.

2017

Never be too prideful to ask for forgiveness. Remember that not every ask will be granted. Your apology shouldn't depend on another person's ability to receive it. If you were wrong, admitting it is your responsibility. Deciding whether or not you will be forgiven is the right of the person that you have wronged.
Your humility and maturity should be tied to your actions, not the reactions your experience as a result.

■ ■ ■ ■ ■

2015

Do the people around you inspire you? Whether friends or family, if you aren't motivated and guided toward greatness by the people that are in your presence each day, adjustments need to be made. Make edits and do so with urgency. Your well-being is dependent on it.

■ ■ ■ ■ ■

2014

Closure is a luxury. It is not a necessity for the faithful. The moment we make it one, we aren't truly having faith in our creator's decisions. There is often entitlement that comes with feeling that you must understand why something happened before you accept it. Faith tells me I must move forward, even if I have to do so blindly. I ask my creator to heal my heart and to remind me that there is a reason for every season. That I may not always get the closure I sometimes feel I desperately need. With this awareness, I can never truly be abandoned.

■ ■ ■ ■ ■

2013

The most difficult part of moving forward after you have been wronged is ensuring the pain inside of you doesn't cause harm to others. It takes effort and courage to break the cycle.

The Forgiveness Mantra

I descend from royalty; my behavior should reflect that at all times.

7
Self-care

2016

Letter to Myself
(Written as my family received news of my Dad's spread of Stage 4 cancer.)

Dear Self,
Wellness begins today!
I'm declaring new healthy habits.
From this moment on I vow to do the following.
If I am interrupted or distracted, I will forgive myself and move forward in my journey.
Put your creator first
Prioritize the rest
Workout daily
Pray and mediate every morning and every night
Limit Social media participation
Read & write

Take vitamins
Drink more water
Decrease sugar intake
Don't take things personally
Don't try to be super woman
Don't internalize
Rid yourself of unnecessary weight
Consider resuming therapy
Make lists of things to do & celebrate tasks once completed
In bed by 11pm
Rise by 5:30am
Exfoliate
Listen to Jazz & Neo Soul music - it soothes and grounds you
Call your Dad - He makes your day
Tell the people close to you that you need their prayers/thoughts
If questions are asked, be honest and forthcoming
Be honest with your loved ones about how scared you are
and about how much pain you're in.
When you want to give up, DON'T!
Celebrate your work ethic and hard work
Be honest, with yourself and others regarding physical limitations, expectations, goals etc.
Forgive
Know when to ask for forgiveness
Be patient with self as these things take a change
Watch meaningful documentaries/ television
Listen to podcasts that are informative and helpful

Listen/watch things that will make you laugh and allow you to pause momentarily
Remember self-preservation is key.
Take care of you. Listen to your mind, body and spirit
Know when to walk away from a conversation or situation
Pray
Stretch
Get massaged
Heal
Be grateful and thank your creator often for all that he has done and will do
Follow your soul
Listen to what the universe is trying to tell you
Walk in faith; know that you are being carried when you cannot walk any longer.

2015

Codependency
(Blog on IamKiaWoods.com & Audio on soundcloud.com/Kia-Woods)

I'm a recovering co-dependent.
That was by far the most honest, vulnerable and scariest sentence I've ever released to the public. It's not a general statement. It is very personal. I've never said it aloud. Even as I'm writing this, I'm questioning my over-sharing. I'm channeling courage in this very moment to release an important piece of myself in an attempt to help someone else.
Many of us are looking to be saved. Without realizing how dependent we are, we look to others around us to validate us. Personally, I battled this for the majority of my adult life. At a certain point I was able to recognize the codependency within, but did not feel there was much that could be done about it. It wasn't until recently that I decided that I no longer wanted to depend on others to feel good about myself. This was a life changing decision.
As an intelligent, out spoken and fairly attractive woman, I have never had an issue attracting a mate or partner. I found myself in relationship after relationship looking for something that I would never find. I didn't know this then, but I was looking for answers. I was looking to feel good about myself. To be told I was good enough, that I was worth it and that the unfortunate experiences of my childhood did not determine

who I was going to be as an adult. I told myself these things daily but I didn't believe my own words. What I was looking for in these encounters with my partners was discovered much later. I was looking to be saved in a sense. Saved from my past and saved from myself.
No one can wash away the pain you have endured. No one can release the garbage that has piled up inside of you just by loving you. There is no love that is great enough without self-love. We all want to be loved and accepted. The truth is, we must do the work to love and accept ourselves if we even want a chance at receiving and appreciating this from others. We enter relationships (both romantic and platonic) seeking to be paired up with someone that just gets it. Sometimes we are successful and we will meet someone that gets us. But if we haven't done the work on ourselves, what they are getting from us, may be less than they deserve. Or perhaps, we end up staring at a reflection of ourselves. Staring at someone who also has a lot of work to do.
So what work have I done? In addition to writing my first book filled with positive statements to absorb each day, I have also been to therapy. What I've learned there, is that piling the good without ever releasing the bad is like spraying air freshener at a dumpster site. It's only briefly masking the root cause. So every day I do the work. I write about the scary things. I speak about them. I confront them. I look myself in the mirror and decide that I am going to be the best

person I know how to be despite the mood I am in that may be telling me to withdraw. I am choosing to have a voice. Release any guilt or shame I have for circumstances I couldn't control. Forgive myself for those I did have control over. Most importantly, I am working on forgiving those whom have hurt me. This is much easier said than done. It all is a CONSTANT and CONTINUOUS work in progress.

Another important thing I am doing is spending time alone. I had to teach myself to like myself before loving myself was even an option. I am for the first time in my life enjoying my own company. I have found solace in my solitude. I enjoy being alone and working out, reading, listening to podcasts, or even just running errands. This is something that's foreign to me. I am not in constant need of company. I love my friends dearly, and I want them around when I am around them. But when I am alone, I am not sad about it. I actually look forward to getting home, lighting candles, running a nice bubble bath and pouring a glass of wine or a cup of tea. Though this may sound simple and even boring to many, to someone that is a recovering codependent, this is a huge step in self-discovery.

Additionally, I have decided that I will not enter another romantic committed relationship any time soon. This has posed challenges and I don't assume they will get easier, as I am still dating and spending quality time with someone I care about. I believe my journey to self-discovery is crucial to my identity. I need to get to know myself and that means I need to be committed to no one other than myself. I need to be in a relationship with me, as I've never truly been committed to all aspects of my development. Sure I've worked hard in school and then in my corporate career. Sure I've sharpened my artistic skills and have been blessed with the ability to create and the drive to push through hardships and uncertainty to share my work.

When it comes to self-care however, I have quite a bit of work to do. I have realized that despite the strength that I have had to acquire, I have still been searching for a hero.

I am now working to become my own.

Homework: Write a letter to anyone that's ever hurt you.

Note: Write the letter whether they are deceased or living. You do not have to send them if you do not want to.

Get every detail down about what they did to you and how they made you feel. Candidly describe their actions and what they have taken from you. Talk about the state of mind you are in as a result and reveal anything you may now be lacking. Get it all out and then do the hardest thing. Promise to forgive them.

Not necessarily right away or not because they even deserve it. Work on it daily until it becomes your truth.

Do it because you deserve to be liberated. Do it because you deserve to be open to receiving love and capable of giving it. Do it because you deserve to love and be loved by YOU!

2017 New Year Resolution

"What if you dedicate the next year to loving yourself?"

Seems like a very simple task when you see it on paper. However, for many of us it is surprisingly difficult. There is usually a list of things we try to tackle with the onset of the New Year. Those things are sometimes beautiful and necessary. But what if we started with loving ourselves more? What if this was our top priority and a goal we pursued wholeheartedly and consistently?

EVERYTHING ELSE WOULD LIKELY FALL INTO PLACE!

YOU CAN complete everything on your to do list.

YOU CAN vibrate higher than you ever have before.

YOU CAN develop resilience against anything or anyone that tries to tear you down or stand in your way.

YOU CAN set intentions and manifest your destiny.

YOU CAN excel in every way you plan to and all the ways you deserve to.

All of this would be easier, even effortless if you begin with self-care.

YOU CAN BE EXCEPTIONAL!

Dedicate this year to loving yourself more than you ever have before, and watch your life transform.

2016

Do more of what makes you healthy and happiness will follow.

2014

It is not only your divine right to ask for what you need, but your responsibility to yourself.

2016

Goals:
Deeper Moments
Genuine connections
Wider prospective
Abandonment of beliefs that weigh me down
Adoption of beliefs that are life bringing
Limit time spent on anything that does not result in magic

2016

Manifestation: The art of falling in love with a future reality.

2014

It is my aim to make spreading love a priority. I extend myself to others not out of obligation but because by being a blessing I am fulfilled.

■ ■ ■ ■ ■

2017

Do not carry the weight of the world simply because you are so used to doing so. Make a commitment to yourself to break old habits. Become the person you want your children to be. Your story isn't over yet. Take control of your life and declare your outcome. Don't spend any more time suffering just because you're used to doing so. It is likely that you have stripped your reality of its abnormality. You CAN want more. You CAN achieve more. So far you have survived, now it is time thrive!

■ ■ ■ ■ ■

2016

Reflect daily.
Reflection and introspection is essential for progression.

Self-care Mantra

I understand that I cannot care for others until I have taken care of myself.
I will make myself a top priority.

8
Strength & Resilience

2015

We sometimes have the need to believe in our own exceptionality. We want to believe that certain things happen only to other people. That we will somehow escape standard consequences of our actions or decisions. Some rules have no exceptions. If you throw something up, it will surely come down. The energy you put out into the universe will always come back around.

2014

Aspire to be a student of life.
Growth should be intentional. Mediocrity is devastating.
Do not accept that you have learned all you are going to learn.
Do not accept that you are unable to move beyond your current situation.
Reject low level thinking meant to stifle you.
While it is important to have an understanding of your foundation, you should be working to consistently develop.

2014

You are much stronger than you realize. When you are in a tough spot, reach deep down, find the strength you need and remind yourself that your current situation isn't your final destination.

2014

Aligning your choices with your intelligence is the very best thing you can do after following your heart has led to disappointment.

2016

Pain that eventually brings forth understanding is called wisdom when it produces a shift in mindset.

2015

Just because you have a right to say something, doesn't mean you shouldn't be selective about when to say it, how to say it and whether to say it at all. Pick your battles. Allow your words to be guided by the light within.

2012

Wise and compassionate souls know that they do not have to relate in order to understand.

2014

Extraordinary people have a gift that allows them to rise above ordinary people and things. They have a responsibility to themselves and to others. They do not think or behave in ways that compromise their exclusivity. If you are aiming to be extraordinary, you must keep this in mind with every encounter.

2013

When adversity pays a visit and causes you to modify your plans, remember to stick to your purpose and never surrender your dreams.

2015

Be grateful for the struggles you've overcome in your lifetime. They are the reason you can now consider yourself a warrior.

2015

Write your remarkable legacy with carefully selected words and actions. The encounters you have today determine the memories you leave behind tomorrow.

Strength & Resilience Mantra

The struggle I have faced in my lifetime has introduced me to strength I wouldn't otherwise have. I have survived!

9
Growth & Wisdom

2014

There is no success without hard work.
We tend to give up prematurely due to the erroneous belief that there is an easier route to something better. I've learned that nothing great comes easy. It is simply a matter of who and what is worth your effort. Life is sometimes hard, confusing, disappointing and unpredictable, but a champion is in search of victory rather than the easy way out.

YOU have been made perfect in your imperfections, strong in your weakest moments and wise in those that require guidance. Some things come naturally. The difficult part is when you excel at what doesn't come easily. Be remarkable ON PURPOSE. Be exceptional BY CHOICE. Elevate beyond your natural height and shine brighter than your natural light. Do the work and take action on things that require effort.

2014

If you aren't aiming for legendary, you are selling yourself short.

2015

To be determined to succeed means to ensure that every choice you make is an investment in your future.

2015

Vibrate at such a high frequency that individuals aspire to elevate simply to get to know you.

2016

Beware: As your vibration rises, forces will come to work against you. Your spiritual awakening will intimidate sleepers. Your increase is a threat to those that need you to remain low functioning. Guard your power!

2015

Be intentional about what you allow to dwell in your mind, for every thought is a seed planted.

2016

I do not know whether there is a God that resides in the sky, or whether there is a spirit occupying the entire universe.
I only know that I know nothing and that I need to be guided by a higher power that is the creator of all things. I accept that power in whatever form.

2016

It's nearly impossible to create a "new you" in the same setting, around the same people, doing the same things.
LEVEL UP! VIBRATE HIGHER!

GROWTH & WISDOM MANTRA

I am remarkable **ON PURPOSE!**

I am exceptional **BY CHOICE!**

10
Discovery - The Things I Have Learned

2016

(In reference to my decision to stop processing my hair, the second time)

I realized the world was profiting off of my insecurities. These were not insecurities that I personally developed but were fed to me from birth. I was tired of it. I wanted to break the cycle. And so, I decided I was beautiful as is. I am a Black woman, in a small frame with brown skin and kinky hair. From this point on, I will not wish to be anything else or have any other features than the ones I was born with. My goal is only to have healthy hair, healthy skin, healthy body, a healthy spirit and a healthy mindset.

2014

All that you are searching for already lives within. Dig Deeper.

2015

It is your responsibility to ensure your actions align with your goals. Beware of all distractions. Limit the time you spend on people and things that are not conducive to the pursuit of your purpose.

2013

I want the legacy I leave behind to be simple. When people think of me after I have left this earth, I want them to say, "She was glorious. She was a warrior."

2014

Sometimes things go wrong for the right reasons. It's either not your time, it's not your route, or it is not intended for your next chapter.

2016

And then suddenly it hit me.
If I wanted a new life, I would have to be willing to sacrifice my old one. I needed to remind myself that not everyone can grow and go with me. As difficult as it was, I had to be willing to end the chapter and turn the page.

2017

If you are a person with a glowing aura, people will undoubtedly be drawn to you. You may not always understand the attraction. Sometimes you may resist it. There may be people that are envious of the admiration and love offered to you by others. They may try to make you feel bad about being a person that is widely loved and respected. Recognize their erroneous way of thinking. Do not apologize for your attractive energy. Do not be manipulated! It is not your responsibility to make others feel comfortable with their mediocrity.

2014

Pain is a part of life.
However, it doesn't have to be life in totality. I've learned that pain has purpose. There is something in it that teaches you, prepares you and/or adds to who you are destined to evolve into. I aim to always work to extract the lesson in pain. Then

and only then, will I know, I have not suffered in vain.

■ ■ ■ ■ ■

2017

I know I have evolved because I made the decision to no longer seek acceptance. I will never again stand in the shadows hoping to blend in. I will not try to explain the intricacies of my layers in hopes of being more relatable. I embrace the differences people will see when they look at me. I will not conform to what will make others more comfortable or what is easy to define. I will not fit into the boxes that have been built to comprehend my complexity. I am a lady but I can also be vulgar. I am receptive but I can also be very stubborn. I am a sensitive empath but I can turn ice cold after I am pushed too far. I am a corporate professional and I am also an independent artist. I am a motivator and I am also a work in progress. I believe in one true love and I also believe in genuine love exchanged through multiple energies. I believe in a higher power but prefer dim lighting, soothing music and meditation at home over going to church or mosque. I am both predictable and a bit of a wild card. I depend on routine but I am excited by spontaneity. I don't own a bible but I believe in the power of prayer. I believe in both nature and nurture. I am a light bringer and also a zealous light seeker. I am proud of the person I am and the range that I offer. No part of me shall be

stifled.
Who I am doesn't have to make sense to you.
Approval is not required. Respect however, is non-negotiable.

* * * * *

2013

Life throws unexpected blows; people will leave you, hurt you and disappoint you.
Things will happen that you may never understand. You'll have many moments of self-doubt. You'll ask why and may even think to yourself that life isn't fair.
At the end of the day, you have two choices:
Be Miserable or Be Motivated.
Each day, no matter how low I may be feeling, I put all I have into my choice.
I am choosing to be motivated!
What choice are you making?

* * * * *

2017

There are times in your life where you won't be able to determine whether the enemy was effective or the universe has been protective. Either way, you have the responsibility to believe you're covered and ensure you respond in a way that doesn't negatively impact your karma.

* * * * *

2017

Being spiritual, positive and progressive doesn't mean you are a perfect person.
It doesn't mean you don't get angry.
It doesn't mean you are never offended and it doesn't mean you won't offend.
It doesn't mean you don't make mistakes.
It doesn't mean you aren't flawed.
It doesn't mean you aren't still growing.
It also doesn't mean that you have to accept mistreatment or remain accessible to people just to prove you've forgiven them.
What it means is that you learn to exit an unfavorable situation before it gets worse.
It means you do not say things out of spite to hurt someone just because they have hurt you.
It means you apologize when you have wronged someone, even if it was unintentional.
It means you do not behave maliciously toward someone just because you no longer see eye to eye.
It means you remain protective of them even when they have displayed behavior that is unsatisfactory.
It means you aren't too proud to say you were wrong.
It means you forgive for your own sanity, even if you choose not to rebuild the relationship.
It means avoiding the harsh things that may come to mind during an argument because you know that hurting someone else will do nothing for you.

It means you will be hurt and confused by malice instead of being vindictive.
It means you do not allow the demons of others to bring out the worst in you.
It means you choose attempting to bring them into your peace instead of allowing them to bring you into their storm.
The high road is a road less traveled, but cannot be avoided on the journey to elevation.

Discovery Mantra

I am glorious!
I am a warrior!

About The Author

Kia Woods was born in New York City. At 12 years old, she began writing poetry and competing in local poetry contests. In 2004, she earned a place on the *Youth Speaks NY* poetry team and competed on a national level in Los Angeles. As a result of this accomplishment, Kia is one of the youngest poets to have performed at *Nuyorican Poets Café* in NYC.

In 2015, Kia released her first book titled ***Positive Reinforcement: Daily Declarations***. Derived from overcoming a tough time in her life, this project included a motivational message for each day of the year. While poetry is her first love, Kia feels it is her calling to inspire a positive mindset while encouraging and engaging her audience.

Kia currently resides in Phoenix, AZ where she also maintains a corporate career. She hopes to one day write and make inspirational speaking appearances on a full time basis.

IAmKiaWoods.com

Soundcloud.com/Kia-Woods

Positive Reinforcement:
Daily Declarations
Kia Amy Woods

1,000 Roads To Discovery

March

March 1:

I am fortunate to have the ability to step outside of myself and see my life, my traits and my habits the way they are viewed by the mass majority. I am able to take personal inventory and discover where I have room to improve — even if the improvement is needed on what may not initially seem to be a problem for me. There is always room for growth and I am thankful for not only how far I've come, but for all that I have left to conquer.

March 2:

I am thankful for the possibilities this new day brings me.

I am anticipating being great on this day. Joy is contagious and I will therefore help others see the potential of the day. My spirits are high and my impact is strong.

I make a difference.

March 3:
Opportunities exist all around me. I have the power to improve my overall happiness by taking advantage of resources I am exposed to and/or by seeking out new ones. I am able-bodied and strong willed. No task is too great when it pertains to my peace of mind. It is always the right time to take a step in the right direction.

March 4:
I am a student of life. I never pass up the opportunity to learn something new. I am grateful and receptive to new information and the expansion of my mind. Knowledge is power.
I am knowledgeable and therefore I am powerful.

March 5:

I value the lives of others.

There are people in my life worthy of every ounce of love I have to offer. I make time for those who make time for me. The people I love know that I love them not only because of words I have spoken, but also because of the message delivered by my actions.

March 6:

I am a giver of the support that I receive and deliver the consistency that I expect from those around me. I do not allow myself to be used by anyone who does not have my best intentions in mind. I use wisdom and discernment when it comes to selecting those people that are close to me. I give and so, I shall receive.

March 7:

Despite my best efforts and judgments, I am wrong at times. When this happens, I am not too prideful to apologize to those I may have affected. I am capable of humbling myself and I am capable of forgiving myself. Additionally, I know that just as I have been wrong, others will be too. I am capable of forgiveness and appreciate humility offered by others.

March 8:

There will not always be perfect days, but there is joy waiting to be discovered in every day. I am able to see the beauty in people, places and things. I live my life with my eyes and my heart wide open.

Great energy flows to and from me freely. Each day is a new opportunity to appreciate being alive.

March 9:

Love is a part of me.

Pain I've endured at the hands of others has not blocked my ability to love. I love others as I want to be loved and I accept, as I would like to be accepted. I steer clear of judgment because I do not want to be judged. I know that what I expect is what I am obligated to reflect.

March 10:

I recognize the power of gratitude.

I understand that although I may not have all of the things that I want, things that are taken for granted can be taken away in an instant. I trust that all that is meant for me will be provided to me. I have faith in timing. As I wait, I work and remain grateful every step of the way for the strength to keep pushing forward.

March 11:

There are choices to make at every turn. I listen to my instinct while also applying logic and channeling wisdom. I am deliberate rather than impulsive. When there is a time I realize I could have made a better choice, I am sure to store the lesson for future reference. By acknowledging that I'll never lose the right to choose, I am beckoning prosperity.

March 12:

Positive energy is contagious.

I receive the positive vibes around me. I use my acquired energy to block negativity. I am eager to pass on positivity as I have encounters with others.

I make connections with people that are pleasant, genuine, memorable and unique in their own way. As I go through my day, I vow to leave behind a trail of positive energy that others are able to thrive on.

March 13:

I am worthy of greatness. I am capable of being great.

No one is able to convince me otherwise or treat me like I am less than a prize.

March 14:

When light from within shines brightly, there will be times when it shines into the eyes of others. My growth will not be stunted, nor will my voice be silenced.

My inner light cannot be dimmed. It reflects far and wide and does so unapologetically.

March 15:

I understand that what happened yesterday has helped to shape who I am today.

With this understanding, I am determined to retrieve the very best that each experience has to offer. From the unfortunate events of the past, I have extracted strength and wisdom. From the joyful times, I have extracted humility and gratitude. Thanks to both the good and bad times, I've walked away armed with exactly what I need for progression.

March 16:

I aspire to the highest forms of achievement in all I do.

March 17:

I am good at many things. I am better at others.

Whether natural talent or something I have to work for,

I do my very best.

There is no room for mediocrity in my life. I'll go to bed satisfied knowing that I've put my best foot forward today.

March 18:

I understand that without true love for myself, it is impossible to fully love another. Self-love and self-worth are blueprints for what I am able to offer the world.

March 19:

There are people who have hurt or left me. Though sad and confused in the moment, I know that I am truly better off without the presence of anyone that doesn't serve me well. I am thankful for what once seemed like misfortune, as I realize it was only a blessing in disguise. I feel protected from harm and prepared for the best years, memories and people of my life. I now understand "losing" someone or something, may not be a loss at all. The universe sometimes makes room in your life for what will be your biggest win!

March 20:

There is nothing that I cannot do if I put my mind to it.

I believe in myself even when others doubt me.

March 21:

There is a beautiful, loving and powerful energy that flows through me. Each day I make the decision to pass along the gift of positivity and to leave a lasting impression on the souls who I encounter.

March 22:

I embrace the many phases life has to offer.

Through the journey of life, I have continuously evolved. The past looks differently than the present just as tomorrow is brand new.

I understand that change is inevitable. I am excited about growth to come. There are many seasons of our lives and I have the strength and courage to adapt to all of them.

March 23:

I have been hurt.

I have stared fear in the face.

I have been torn and I have been broken.

I have scars that serve as evidence that I fought and survived. I vow to turn all my wounds into wisdom.

March 24:

I have learned that I want to never stop learning.

I am a student of life.

The world is my classroom and life is my teacher.

March 25:

It is natural for me to want to take care of others. I am a one-person support system when I need to be. I take the time to take care of myself so that I can be at my best. I know that my love for others should not come before self-preservation. Taking care of me, means that I am doing a favor to those who depend on me.

March 26:

Today is a brand new day. Any negativity of yesterday has been cancelled out. Today I am choosing my attitude very carefully. I will check in with myself periodically and make adjustments as needed. Happiness is mine for the taking. No one or nothing can bring me down without my permission. Anyone intending to do so will promptly be denied access!

March 27:

Life is sometimes fast-paced. We often get so busy that we forget to take the time to meditate, reflect and appreciate the moment. I am vowing to slow down when I feel life passing me by. I promise to meditate on words that motivate me, reflect on my behavior and decisions, and appreciate all of my blessings.

March 28:

I will not be held captive by regret. Life has taught me many things that I will value for the rest of my days. I move on knowing there is a purpose in my pain and that if I extract the lesson, I have not suffered in vain.

March 29:

Love flows through me freely.

I am able to love without reservation and hesitation. At times, I have to love from a distance. When that decision is made, it isn't because my heart is hardened, but because I am protecting my river of love from pollution.

March 30:

Confidence dwells within me.

It is stronger than my insecurities, and more solid than my doubts. I know that I am working continuously to be all that I am meant to be. Though undoubtedly a work in progress, the person I see in the mirror is phenomenal just by aspiring to greatness. I am on my way!

March 31:

Blessings are all around me.

I may not have all that I want, but I am grateful to have all that I need. I am happy to celebrate the success of others, knowing that I am successful in my own right.

I do not envy what others have. Instead, I focus on the great things in my life and work toward goals that will land me in the place meant especially for me.

April

April 1:

Today I will have no complaints. I will not speak ill of others, nor will I put myself down. I will dedicate time to simply say thank you for waking up this morning, for the food I will consume, for the clothing I will wear and for air that I will breathe all day. I will check on the people I love today. I will remember that their lives are important to me, and one more reason to make this a day of gratitude.

April 2:

I am encouraged.

I speak victory into my life. It only takes one life changing moment to place me in a space of greatness beyond my own imagination. I will ensure I have an attitude that is prepared and deserving to receive the blessings in store.

April 3:

I surround myself with people that lift me higher.

April 4:

I am invested in sharing my strengths and my talent.

I understand that a gift is truly not a gift until it is given.

April 5:

My energy is magnetic.

I draw in those with similar vision of peace, knowledge and understanding. I patiently wait for meaningful connections to be made with beautiful beings. I embrace and cherish relationships approved by the universe.

April 6:
I have the ability to soar beyond my imaginary limitations. Only I have the ability to hinder myself. My journey cannot be defined by anyone's standards or beliefs. I will not be controlled by fear. It is my mission to disprove all doubt that lives within. I will keep climbing until I have reached the high that is predestined for me.

April 7:
Paths will cross and paths will split. When someone exits my life, I will not mourn the will of the universe. I understand that I was whole before them and that I will be whole again.

April 8:

I am patient with others and I am patient with myself.

I understand that we are all human beings made up of flawed pieces of perfection. My expectations are that the people around me try their best, and I vow to do the same. When a mistake is made, I am able to ask for forgiveness and I am able to grant forgiveness as well.

April 9:

I have the power and strength to release what no longer serves me. Anything that does not add to my purpose, foster growth or keep me whole shall be kept at a distance.

April 10:

I am grateful for life.

I've seen my share of ups and downs, but the good times outweigh the bad by far.

I approach this new day with excitement.

April 11:

The power to choose means that I am in control.

I am able to choose my attitude. I work hard to see the good in people. I can see the bright side of every situation. I am making the choice to extract the lesson when things happen that bring my spirits down. Therefore, I am choosing positivity even at my lowest moments.

April 12:

The word "if" will be removed from my vocabulary.

In regard to goal setting, I am interested only in "when" I will achieve them.

April 13:

I am strong. I am powerful. I am resilient.

My spirit is renewed on command.

Positivity is channeled at my will.

All tools needed for success of the day are stored within.

April 14:
Today will be a good day.
I will recognize new opportunities as they present themselves. Negativity and conflict will not be acknowledged. The tone has been set. Positive vibrations have been released.

April 15:
The celebration of life will be my focus today.
I celebrate my own life and lives of my loved ones.
My soul is comforted knowing that they have also lived to see a new day. Just as I want to be loved and appreciated as I dwell on earth, I will ensure I show my love and appreciation for these precious lives while they are here.

Tonight I will rest easy knowing that meaningful relationships have been nurtured.

April 16:
Just as sun rises and gives the day meaning, I rise this morning ensured that my life is meaningful.
I have a purpose and I am dedicated to living it.

April 17:
I have the courage to re-evaluate and reconstruct pieces of my life.
What once belonged in my life, may not any longer.
I accept that.
I will not hold on to what should not be mine or what never was.

April 18:
Energy will leave my soul and attach to the souls of others in every encounter I have today. I will ensure that it is positive energy. Be it casual conversation, physical contact or a meeting of the minds, my imprint will be memorable. My remarkable legacy is being written.

April 19:
I am encouraged. I am more than a conqueror. I cancel out all doubt. As it is believed, it will come to be. I speak victory into existence on this day and the ones to come.

April 20:

I am beautiful. I am heroic in my own right. I am a leader, a humanitarian, and a motivator. I give freely and so, I shall receive in abundance. I am a blessing to others and therefore, I am blessed.

April 21:

My time is precious.

My energy is reserved for the deserving.

Every moment that passes is a moment I will never live again.

Today I vow to choose my battles wisely.

I am dedicated to directing my attention to what and who really matters in my life.

April 22:

I summon all that I need today.

I will attract the energy and mindset to be at peace on this day. I call for strength and resilience as needed. I ask to be filled with joy so magical it works through me and is passed on to others. I hope for awareness that allows me to identify each and every blessing, even while they are in the making.

April 23:

Greatness dwells within me and is applied to everything that I do. I choose the right way, even when it's not the easy way. Those who know me would testify that I am an exceptional person. I stand tall and proud at the end of each day knowing that I've done my very best.

April 24:

I have the strength to let go of what and who no longer serves me. If it isn't conducive to my continuous progression, it shall be cancelled out.

April 25:

I am a protector of my loved ones. Though I am unable to protect them from all they will see in this world, my presence in their lives means they will hurt a little less, smile a little more and never feel alone. I forgive myself for any time I've fallen short in the past. I move forward today with a brand new shield of love.

April 26:

When decisions are difficult and roads are unclear,

when I am fighting battles both internal and external, when I am uncertain, I follow peace.

April 27:
I am thankful for each night that has turned into a new morning, each friend that has turned into a new family member, and each dream that has turned into reality. I am grateful for all that I have today Everything that I need has been provided. I will not take this day for granted. I live and love in appreciation.

April 27:
I act, walk, speak and live with intent. Everything I do is done with purpose. All that I am is meaningful.

April 28:

I will not be weighed down.

I am light.

I am free.

I am at peace.

April 29:

I am in need of no outside validation. I am able to reward myself for a job well done. I will take the time to treat myself because I know I deserve it.

I am more than worthy.

April 30:

I am strong, I am powerful, and I am resilient. I will not be broken. As wounds heal, the scars left behind are a reminder that I have survived.

www.ingramcontent.com/pod-product-compliance
Lightning Source LLC
Chambersburg PA
CBHW032122090426
42743CB00007B/433